Baby Dot

A Dinosaur Story

by Margery Cuyler

illustrated by Ellen Weiss

Clarion Books

New York

Pen and ink and watercolor were used
to create the full-color artwork.
The text type is 16 pt. ITC Zapf International Light.

Clarion Books
a Houghton Mifflin Company imprint
215 Park Avenue South, New York, NY 10003
Text copyright © 1990 by Margery Cuyler
Illustrations copyright © 1990 by Ellen Weiss

For information about permission to reproduce
selections from this book, write to Permissions,
Houghton Mifflin Company, 2 Park Street, Boston, MA 02108.
Printed in the USA

Library of Congress Cataloging-in-Publication Data
Cuyler, Margery.
Baby Dot / by Margery Cuyler ; illustrated by Ellen Weiss.
p.   cm.
Summary: After failing to adjust well to the routines of the
learning cave and refusing to go back, spoiled girl dinosaur Baby
Dot finally returns and encounters another young dinosaur even
meaner than she was.
ISBN 0-395-51934-9
[1. Dinosaurs—Fiction.   2. Schools—Fiction.   3. Behavior—
Fiction.]   I. Weiss, Ellen, ill.   II. Title.
PZ7.C997Bab   1990   89-77726
[E]—dc20   CIP
                                      AC

H O R 10 9 8 7 6 5 4 3 2 1

For Thomas, with love
—M.C.

To Mollie, with love
—F.W.

Baby Dot lived in a stony cave with Mama, Papa, Bert, and Gertie. Bert and Gertie looked like other little dinosaurs, but Baby Dot was different. She was covered with polka dots.

Mama and Papa thought Baby Dot
was beautiful. Every afternoon, they took
her for a walk.

"What a precious baby," their neighbors
said. Baby Dot grinned.
Mama and Papa beamed.

But Bert and Gertie thumped their tails.
"She's not all that precious," they said.

As Baby Dot grew, Mama and Papa let her do whatever she wanted. Soon, she got spoiled.

She bellowed when she wanted trees and cones.

She crushed Bert and Gertie's sticks and bones.

She grabbed their rocks and stones.

One day, when Baby Dot was taking a nap,
Bert and Gertie ran to Mama and Papa.

"Baby Dot's mean," said Bert.

"Baby Dot's bad," said Gertie.

"Baby Dot's different," said Papa. "It's not
every day one has a polka-dot baby."

"Even so," said Mama, "Baby Dot *is* bad
sometimes. Just yesterday, she pulled up all the
trees in front of the cave."

"Maybe it's time to send her to school,"
said Papa.

Bert and Gertie thumped their tails. "We
don't want Baby Dot at school," they said.

"Nonsense," said Mama. "School will be
good for her."

The next morning, Mama and Papa took
their children to the learning cave.

"This is Baby Dot," they told Mrs. Crocodile.
"Take good care of her!"

They kissed Baby Dot good-bye. "Now be a
good girl," they said. And then they left.

Bert and Gertie ran to the toy corner. They started to play house with the other children.

Baby Dot sat and clutched her blanket.

"Want to come play?" asked Mrs. Crocodile.

"I want to go home!" said Baby Dot.

"Not until school's over," said Mrs. Crocodile.

Mrs. Crocodile handed Baby Dot a doll. Baby Dot threw it on the floor.

Then she put her blanket over her head. She didn't take it off until Mama and Papa came back.

"How was school?" they asked.

"Great!" said Bert.

"Fun!" said Gertie.

But Baby Dot didn't say a thing. She just sulked.

When they got home, Baby
Dot lay on her bed and looked at
the ceiling.

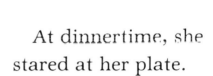

At dinnertime, she
stared at her plate.

At bathtime, she was
very quiet.
"I don't think Baby Dot
likes the learning cave,"
said Papa.
"I'm sure the second
day will be better," said
Mama.

But it wasn't.

After Mama and Papa left, Baby Dot lay down and thumped her tail.

"I want to go home!" she screamed. "I want my mama and papa!" Then she started to cry.

Bert and Gertie were building a toy volcano.
"I wish she'd be quiet!" said Bert.
"She's acting horrible!" said Gertie.
"Don't worry," said Mrs. Crocodile. "She'll
get over it. She just needs to get used to school."

Mrs. Crocodile carried Baby Dot to the painting wall.

"Here are some paints," she said. "Would you like to try using red?"

Baby Dot threw the paint on the floor.

"I want to go home!" she shrieked.

Then she ran to the volcano. She kicked it
hard. All the stones fell down.
"Bad girl!" yelled Bert and Gertie.

Mrs. Crocodile walked Baby Dot to the nap corner.

"You'll have to stay here until you can behave!" she said.

Baby Dot stayed there for the rest of the morning. She was very quiet.

But when she got home,
she was terrible. She threw
rocks and stones.

She crushed sticks
and bones.

She stamped on
trees and cones.

"Enough!" shouted Mama and Papa.
"What's wrong with you, anyway?"
Baby Dot thumped her tail. "I don't
want to go back to school!" she yelled.
"I don't like school!"

"Maybe we should keep you home tomorrow," said Papa.

"Maybe you're too young for school," said Mama.

Bert and Gertie nodded their heads and smiled.

The next day, Bert and Gertie went
to the learning cave by themselves.
Baby Dot stayed home.

She piled up trees
and cones.

She played with
rocks and stones.

She counted sticks and bones.
But she was bored.

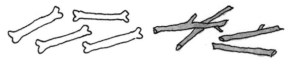

"Come play," she said to Mama and Papa.

But Papa was busy
eating leaves.

Mama was busy
sweeping the cave.

"Maybe later," said Mama.
"Maybe tomorrow," said Papa.

Baby Dot picked up some stones to build a volcano. But it was no fun making a volcano by herself.

She wondered what the children were doing at school.

She walked outdoors to nibble some leaves. She wished Bert and Gertie were there to have a snack, too.

After a while, Baby Dot went and found Mama. She tugged her tail.

"I want to go back to school," she said.

"You do?" asked Mama.

"I do," said Baby Dot.

So the next morning, Mama and Papa took
Baby Dot back to the learning cave.
"I hope Baby Dot's good today," said Bert.
"Me too," said Gertie.

Mrs. Crocodile greeted them at the cave entrance.
"Hi, Baby Dot," she said. "I'm glad you came
back. Come meet Baby Bronto. This is his first
day at school."

A little dinosaur crawled from behind Mrs. Crocodile.

"Hello, Baby Bronto," said Baby Dot.

The little dinosaur took one look at Baby Dot and started to scream. "I want my mama!" he shrieked.

Baby Dot looked at Baby Bronto.

"Nonsense!" she said. She gave him a kiss. Then she grabbed his paw and pulled him toward the toy corner.

"May we play?" she asked
the other children.
"If you're nice," they said.

Baby Dot handed Baby
Bronto a stone.
"Come help build a
volcano," she said.
Baby Bronto threw the stone
on the floor. Then he thumped
his tail and put his blanket over
his head.

"Baby Bronto's mean," said
Bert.
"Baby Bronto's bad," said
Gertie.
"He's not so bad," said Baby
Dot. "He just needs to get used
to school!"

Then she sat down and started building a
volcano with the other little dinosaurs.